PRAYERS
and
PROMISES

PRAYERS and PROMISES

Written by Patti Bazemore

Illustrated by Jade Collins

XULON PRESS

Xulon Press
2301 Lucien Way #415
Maitland, FL 32751
407.339.4217
www.xulonpress.com

Unless otherwise indicated, Scripture quotations taken from (Version(s) used)

Paperback ISBN-13: 978-1-6628-1759-5
Hard Cover ISBN-13: 978-1-6628-1760-1
Ebook ISBN-13: 978-1-6628-1761-8

Dedication

My sweet Heavenly Father – You are my why. You are my writer, my encourager, my reason, and my all in all! I am blown away each day by Your faithfulness and constant love. May this book honor and glorify You, pointing us to the stars and all the places where Your promises are revealed!

Micah John's BigBig – You are my bigger than big. Thank you for your encouragement and support. This book would not have been possible without you. I always have and forever will…love you!

Micah John – When the blue gun powder floated into the air at your gender reveal, I knew that my life would be forever changed by a precious, little boy. I am so thankful God chose you to be that little boy! I love you more than you will ever understand or know this side of heaven.

GRRR

BOING

ZOOM

Micah John loved to go outside. He enjoyed playing with his tractors in the sand, jumping on the trampoline, and riding his bike. But Micah John's favorite thing to do outside was to be with his grandfather, BigBig.

Often when Micah John visited BigBig, the two of them would go outside at night. BigBig would pick the little boy up in his arms, point up to the sky, and the two of them would gaze at the stars together.

One night in particular, the stars were plentiful. As the grandfather and grandson looked up to the heavens, BigBig began to tell Micah John of a beautiful story from long ago.

He told the little boy about a man named Abram, who was a follower of God.

Abram and his wife Sarai wanted to have a baby, but they were both old in age and had given up hope of having children of their own.

One night, God asked Abram to look up to the sky at the many stars. God asked Abram to count the stars, but there were so many that Abram could not count them all.

God made a promise to Abram, telling Abram that he and Sarai would have many children. God told Abram that his children, their children, and their children's children would be so many that like the stars, he would not be able to count them all.

Abram was happy and thanked God for His promise.

BigBig looked at his grandson and told him he had PRAYED for a grandchild for several years. BigBig shared with his grandson about the day he and Micah John's grandmama had heard they would be grandparents. Micah John's mama and daddy had told BigBig and Grandmama they were having triplets.

BigBig still remembered the joy he immediately felt knowing that he would be a grandfather. He told Micah John that God had answered his prayer for a grandchild when Micah John and his two sisters had been born. Micah John stared into the eyes of his grandfather and smiled.

BigBig gently lowered the little boy to the ground, held his hand, and the two of them walked across the yard to the house next door where Micah John lived.

As the two approached the house, they walked up the steps to the porch and stopped. BigBig knelt in front of Micah John, stretched his arms tightly around him, and hugged him closely. As BigBig held Micah John securely in his arms, BigBig began to pray: "Father in heaven, thank you for Your promises and for answering our prayers. We understand that our prayers are not always answered in the ways we would like, but we know that You answer each prayer in the way that is best for us.

Thank you for Micah John. Thank you for answering my prayer and giving me a grandson to love and spend time with. Father, please watch over him. May he always know the love I have for him, and, more importantly, may he know Your love. May he always acknowledge and believe in Your promises. Father, we love you. Amen."

BigBig opened the door to Micah John's house. Once he was inside, BigBig told him good night, closed the door, and began to walk back home. As he walked, he looked to the heavens one last time, where the many twinkling stars were scattered throughout. Once again, BigBig thanked God for His answered prayer of the gift of a grandson.

GENESIS 15:5 – "He took him outside and said, 'Look up at the heavens and count the stars—if indeed you can count them.' Then he said to him, 'So shall your offspring be.'"

Follow me on Facebook

Patti Cheek Bazemore
https://www.facebook.com/patti.bazemore

Instagram

@pattibazemore

My Blog

@fromthepicketfencetothecross.com

CPSIA information can be obtained
at www.ICGtesting.com
Printed in the USA
LVHW071000170621
690062LV00014B/213